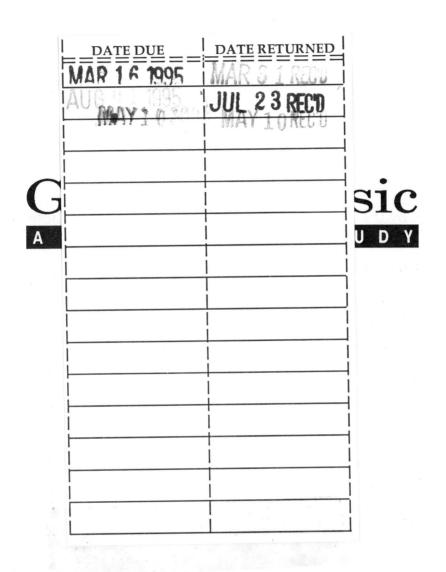

G   sic

A   UDY

MUSIC EDUCATORS NATIONAL CONFERENCE

Developed by the MENC Task Force on General Music Course of Study

Charles R. Hoffer, National Executive Board Liaison

Linda Mercer, Chair
Ray Doughty
Jeffrey Patchen
John Yeager

Copyright © 1991
Music Educators National Conference
1806 Robert Fulton Drive, Reston, VA 22091-4348
All rights reserved.
Printed in the United States of America
ISBN 0-940796-98-8

Contents

The MENC Task Force on General Music Course of Study has compiled *Teaching General Music: A Course of Study* to provide teachers with assistance in developing courses of study. In compiling this material, the Task Force members drew not only on their own training and experience but on that of music educators from across the country.

Rather than a complete or final recommended course of study, this document provides a representative approach that teachers can use in conjunction with the MENC publication *The School Music Program: Description and Standards* to improve the quality of music instruction at all levels. No endorsement of any particular method for music teaching is intended or should be inferred.

Foreword

There is a growing concern in public school education for each discipline to identify learning outcomes appropriate for the ages of children being taught. As a result of this general educational concern, music teachers are being asked to design courses of study in the same manner as teachers in other disciplines. It is reasonable that music educators be held accountable for what is being taught in classrooms and rehearsal halls. It is also reasonable to assume that students can demonstrate what they have learned as a consequence of the instruction delivered.

Teachers often contact MENC for assistance in developing courses of study for local school districts. In the spring of 1988 a meeting was held in conjunction with MENC's National Biennial In-Service Conference in Indiana to explore the development of courses in general music, band, orchestra, and chorus. It was agreed that MENC should proceed in generating such courses of study that could serve as models for any school district in the country. These courses would identify a sequence of outcomes for various ages and/or ability levels of music students.

Teachers with proven records of teaching success were selected to participate in each of the four projects. These educators spent more than two years developing materials simple and concise enough to be helpful for teachers as they plan instruction. Because each instructional area is unique, each committee was free to develop any format it felt appropriate. The four documents were never intended to be a "national" course of study; instead they offer teachers a model for the development of sequenced learning outcomes that meet their local needs.

The documents also reflect input from numerous other outstanding educators who took time to read rough drafts and respond to questionnaires. MENC hopes that teachers will find this document and the other three in the series helpful in administering sequenced music instruction that results in easily measurable learning outcomes.

Donald L. Corbett
Past President, MENC

Introduction

This course of study document is intended to serve as a model for music teachers to use in developing their own curriculum. Objectives and accompanying possible procedures are representative selections of such items, and they should not be considered as a complete list of what can or should be accomplished. Song titles, compositions, and composers are also representative selections. Objectives are arranged sequentially, but any of them may be repeated at a later level.

The format of this publication is derived from *The School Music Program: Description and Standards* (second edition, Music Educators National Conference, 1986). Therefore, objectives and possible procedures are organized under the categories of Performing/Reading, Creating, Listening/Describing, and Valuing. Objectives and possible procedures organized in these categories are appropriate across categories, and any categorical separateness is artificial and primarily for the purpose of organizational simplicity. This experience-based approach to organization of curriculum is a common one for many teachers.

Another approach for organizing objectives is conceptual, grouping objectives according to the concepts or components of pitch, duration, loudness, timbre, texture, form, and style. All music learning—general, choral, instrumental, theory, and appreciation—can be approached by these concepts of music. This organization may be integrated into the experience-based approach, with components appearing in all categories of Performing/Reading, Creating, Listening/Describing, and Valuing.

Participation in the indicated levels of learning assumes that the curriculum is implemented by music educators through regular cumulative experiences.[1] The organization of objectives will need to be adjusted for those situations where scheduling is not sequential or consistent.

Regardless of the organizational structure, all decisions regarding the music curriculum should grow out of a solidly established set of principles and reflect outcomes available to all students. The MENC goals listed on pages 13 and 14 of *The School Music Program: Description and Standards* are useful for guiding music teachers in developing their own goals. An abridged version of the MENC Rationale and Outcome statements follows:

Music is worth knowing. It is a field of study with its own body of knowledge, skills, and ways of thinking. The ability to perform, create, and listen to music with understanding is desirable for every member of society. Studying music transmits cultural heritage, develops each person's musical potential, provides an opportunity for creativity and self-expression, helps students understand the nature of humankind, enables students to become sensitive listeners, cultivates a unique symbol system, and enhances the quality of life.

School music programs should offer students opportunities to develop
- their ability to make music, alone and with others
- their ability to improvise and create music
- their ability to use the vocabulary and notation of music
- their ability to respond to music aesthetically, intellectually, and emotionally
- their understanding of a wide variety of music, including diverse musical styles, cultures, and genres

■ their understanding of the role music has played and continues
   to play in the lives of human beings
■ their ability to make aesthetic judgments based on critical listening and analysis
■ their commitment to music
■ a supportive attitude for the musical life of the community, as
   well as a desire to encourage a supportive attitude in others
■ their ability to continue music learning independently

Evaluation is an essential component of course of study or curriculum planning. Each objective should contain an element of evaluation because students produce or exhibit some musical behavior. Assessing student progress in music learning will indicate levels of student achievement to students, parents, and administrators. It will also indicate whether (1) students can solve musical problems, (2) a teacher's approach is effective, and (3) the objectives are within students' capabilities. Music teachers are encouraged to develop evaluation and assessment procedures that reflect progress in learning musical concepts and to avoid extrinsic elements such as behavior, attendance, or appearance.

1. *The School Music Program: Description and Standards* (Reston, VA: Music Educators National Conference, 1986), 20, 24, 33, 47.

Preschool/Kindergarten

Music learning is especially important during early childhood. Preschool- and kindergarten-aged students are able to accomplish a great deal musically, and they should be encouraged to expand their natural abilities through play and singing games. Research findings indicate that children at this age have a narrow vocal range, but that it can be expanded and developed with encouragement and practice. It is important to begin pitch-matching experiences early with careful attention to listening skills.

These students can understand the concepts of high and low or loud and soft, but they may not use the same vocabulary as adults when expressing the concepts. Rhythmic awareness is also established early, and children should move, clap, stamp, and patsch to a wide variety of pulses. Designated areas of the music room or classroom should be available for exploration and play, and should offer a good collection of music materials and equipment, including instruments and recordings.

Performing/Reading

Objectives

During preschool and kindergarten the student will:

- use singing and speaking voice to demonstrate different vocal timbres

- select and play a variety of classroom instruments to indicate different timbres

- match given pitch patterns through singing within a comfortable range

- sing simple short melodies with a range of a fifth

- respond to a steady beat through clapping, swaying, walking, etc.

- sing or chant an example of loud and soft dynamics through alternating short phrases or echoing

- move to indicate phrase changes in simple form, such as ABA, AA

- play classroom instruments to demonstrate phrase changes

- play or sing high or low pitches given a reference pitch

- sing a variety of simple folk songs and composed songs for the young voice

- create visual representations to indicate formal structure such as three-part (ABA) and two-part (AB)

- create personal icons to represent simple pitch patterns or directions

Possible Procedures

- chant and sing songs and discuss differences in sounds

- sing and play on a variety of pitched and non-pitched instruments, and talk about differences in sounds

- participate in call and response; name games such as "where is..?"

- begin with descending third calls; expand to fifths

- mimic teacher's sequence of duple or triple patterns with echo clapping; move to recorded examples of marches or waltzes

- sing simple songs such as "Row Your Boat," "Are You Sleeping," while alternating loud and soft phrases

- stand and sit at phrase changes or repeated phrases

- alternate rhythm and chord instruments to show phrase changes

- imitate teacher by singing or playing pitched instruments on high and low pitches

- sing rote-learned songs such as "Go Tell Aunt Rhody," "Jump Down, Turn Around"

- use pictures or symbols to represent form, for example: * + *, # >

- draw or arrange felt pieces to represent pitch outlines, such as ascending or descending lines

Objectives	Possible Procedures
◾ compose short pieces demonstrating simple durational patterns	◾ develop symbols for long and short, make patterns from them, and then perform patterns by clapping or by playing on classroom instruments; by using personal icons or symbols for pitch patterns and durational patterns, invent personal "composition"

Creating

Objectives

During preschool and kindergarten the student will:

- invent simple sound patterns

- develop system for communicating individual improvised patterns

- create or invent songs to accompany play or stories

- develop icons to communicate and record personal pieces

- sing or play invented endings to melodic phrase presented

- express mood through movement or classroom instruments

Possible Procedures

- play rhythm or mallet instruments to demonstrate invention

- draw map or create story to demonstrate pattern

- exhibit appropriate behaviors while working or playing in music classroom centers; invent group song to accompany story

- express and record personal musical ideas with teacher assistance

- respond with sung "answer" to "questions" sung by teacher

- choose joyful and angry moods, and express through playing classroom instruments; create movement to express feelings

Listening/Describing

Objectives

During preschool and kindergarten the student will:

- following teacher-guided experiences, listen to short compositions

- move to and discuss components that occur in listening examples

- expand attention to a variety of familiar and unfamiliar music through repeated listenings

- indicate high and low pitches through listening

- move to express contrast of loud and soft dynamic levels

- demonstrate through movement and discuss style characteristics of march and lullaby

- graphically represent "smooth and jumpy"; stepwise movements or skips of a piece

- visually and aurally identify instruments that represent different families such as string, wind, percussion

- talk about musical sounds using simple vocabulary such as up/down, loud/soft, fast/slow

Possible Procedures

- listen to one short selection from collection such as *Carnival of the Animals*, and then talk about how music represents that animal

- select examples of beat, repetition, melody, and speed for discussion; for example, fast/slow, same/different

- listen to brief examples of unfamiliar music, repeating and extending in successive classes

- move hand or arm to show high and low pitches

- stand and sit to demonstrate, or play rhythm instruments on cues for loud and soft

- listen to sample march and lullaby, and then talk about differences; move to demonstrate fast and slow

- draw on chalkboard with wide chalk to represent melodic contour

- point out visual and timbre differences among string, wind, and percussion families through pictures and sound examples

- listen to simple song demonstration (live or recorded) and talk about its characteristics

Valuing

Objectives	Possible Procedures

During preschool and kindergarten the student will:

■ discuss how music exists at home and school

■ participate eagerly in classroom music activities

■ spontaneously use music to accompany private tasks or games

■ select from available recorded music

■ recognize music as work or occupation

■ discuss music event with the family

■ through invented writing or on tape, record information about music events in his or her life into journal

■ join in singing games and listen attentively in class

■ hum or sing to self, turn on recorded music to accompany play

■ pick favorite recording from classroom collections

■ meet local musicians in the classroom; view videos that demonstrate music careers

■ share how music adds to family social, recreational, and spiritual events

Level 1–3

Primary students need many opportunities to continue developing musical skills. Movement is very important at this level to help students internalize the concepts of music. Students at this age are capable of inventing and composing music, and they should be encouraged to do so. The early use of symbols to communicate personal and group musical ideas is essential to developing beginning reading skills. Invented or standardized icons and simplified notation facilitate such communication. Students may produce music through singing or playing instruments, or through computers or other technology. Singing is especially important for continuing the development of vocal range and production.

Responding to music and reflecting upon it are important beginning skills, and they encourage students to value and respect music and their participation in it. At this age it is appropriate to begin developing an understanding of lifelong participation in music. Music selected for learning settings should reflect many cultures or ethnic perspectives.

Performing/Reading

Objectives

During the primary grades the student will:

- demonstrate initial understanding of posture and breathing used to promote good sound while singing

- sing with others or with accompaniment using listening skills to match pitches

- sing several selected songs expressively

- sing or play simple ostinati to accompany songs or rhythm activities

- maintain own part in round or partner song

- move to music demonstrating tempo changes

- demonstrate understanding of note values and patterns

- exhibit awareness of simple and complex rhythm patterns

- read and play, clap, or chant simple rhythm patterns from notation

- play, sing, or move to represent pitch patterns from notation

- "read" unfamiliar songs through observing notation

- sing from notation using syllables, note names, or *la*

Possible Procedures

- Sit or stand with good posture, expand ribs while breathing, sing with a free clear tone, avoiding straining or yelling

- sing in unison with teacher or classmates adjusting pitch to be "in tune"

- select ethnic, patriotic, or holiday songs that contain expressive content: pride, affection, fear, surprise, and so on

- play student- or teacher-prepared *bourdon* on pitched mallet instruments

- sing familiar round melody alone and then with another student as a round

- patsch or clap to fast/slow example

- move to music by stepping, skipping, hopping, or running

- echo clap in imitative or canonic exercise

- read and clap examples from flash cards, chalkboard, or songbook

- "read" sample of short, simple familiar song from chalkboard or overhead transparencies

- determine beat, form, step or skip of melodic line, range, and speed through observation and discussion of printed notation

- try to sing unfamiliar song material after having tonal reference points of scale or I, IV, and V chords presented

Creating

Objectives

During the primary grades the student will:

- sing or play improvised answers to music phrases

- compose short melodic phrases to be played or sung

- create pieces using nontraditional sounds such as environmental or body sounds

- invent pieces or organize sequence of familiar pieces to interpret stories or themes

- create movement to express musical ideas

Possible Procedures

- respond to aural or visual phrase provided by teacher

- use real or invented notation to record; keep compositions in portfolio for future improvement and changes

- collect different-pitched objects from a variety of sources and use for basis for new piece

- select story or theme as a group, and then construct music to express ideas and moods using solos, recitative, and chorus

- select short programmatic piece to demonstrate story or affective response

Listening/Describing

Objectives

During the primary grades the student will:

■ hear and discuss selected components of music

  Pitch: major/minor, tone center

  Duration: fast/slow, long/short, duple/triple

  Loudness: loud/soft, crescendo/ decrescendo, accent

  Form: repeated phrases, contrasting phrases, two-part and three-part form, rondo, canon

■ demonstrate through movement to acknowledge change in pitch

■ plan a series of movements or pictures to represent how a given piece sounds

■ identify families of instruments and individual instruments visually and aurally

■ recognize stylistic characteristics of overall selection

■ identify simple forms (AB, ABA, and canons) through listening

Possible Procedures

■ upon hearing pieces selected by teacher for demonstration

  identify tonal center by singing

  distinguish fast and slow, imitate long and short, recognize music in duple and triple time

  indicate loud and soft through gestures

  upon hearing repetitions, demonstrate through signaling; show formal patterns through icons

■ move hand up and down to indicate interval and step changes

■ after several teacher-guided listenings, develop plan or map and record it for collection in portfolio

■ listen to and examine varieties of instruments and discuss timbral and construction differences

■ listen to and identify examples of religious, folk, classical, Spanish, cowboy, Asian, and African-American music

■ point to call charts or listening maps to identify form changes

Valuing

Objectives

During the primary grades the student will:

■ expand list of places where music occurs in personal lives: home, school, community, festivals, parties, parades, radio, television, movies

■ relate personal incident regarding important role of music to self

■ react to lives of well-known composers

■ participate spontaneously in music endeavors alone or with groups

■ be willing to work at solving "musical problem"

■ select music to listen to with a purpose

■ discuss why music is personally important

Possible Procedures

■ record information in journal regarding music as it occurs in his or her life, using audio taped or written entries

■ talk about sports events, church or temple, TV shows, and cartoons, and describe music's role in each

■ report on appropriate biographical sketches of famous composers; relate anecdotes interesting to age group

■ volunteer to play or sing solos and to participate in group activities

■ exhibit patience and perseverance to perfect personal effort such as composition, recording, or chart

■ recognize the effect of music on attitude, mood, and enjoyment

■ talk about preferences with guidance from teacher about relating to music concepts

Level 4–6

Students in grades 4–6 should have the basic music knowledge to begin exploring and manipulating the components of music. Music reading skills can be achieved at this level, and students may further develop their reading skills through singing or by playing a keyboard or other classroom instruments. As students compose or improvise their own or group ideas, they will become proficient in using music notation and symbols.

Creative endeavors may extend to movement to express patterns, form, or melodic contour and to drama for interpreting and expressing musical ideas. Listening to and reflecting on live or recorded music becomes a more integral part of the students' experiences at this level. Continued opportunities to explore and express a variety of personal and ethnic perspectives should be included. Through field trips and video/film recordings students gain more insight into the many career opportunities in music.

Performing/Reading

Objectives

During the intermediate grades the student will:

- sing independently, demonstrating an open, free vocal quality

- sing independently from notation, observing pitch, rhythmic, and stylistic symbols

- maintain individual part during the singing of canons, partner songs, or rounds

- sing harmonies of thirds and fifths at cadences by ear

- play notated or created rhythmic and tonal patterns on classroom instruments such as recorder, keyboard, or synthesizer

- play simple music from notation on selected classroom instruments

- accompany class songs on chord instruments (Autoharp, electronic keyboard, guitar) by ear, and from notation

- move to or conduct duple and triple meters

- perform from music notation, indicating understanding of form directives

- perform folk dances representative of various cultures

Possible Procedures

- produce "solo" performance using a "mike" to enhance realism; class may provide accompaniment

- with teacher's help, scan new piece, identifying clues such as key signatures, time signatures, tempo, range, and note values

- sing in duets or trios to demonstrate ability to maintain own part

- imitate vocal and instrumental examples of harmony

- play walking bass, *bourdon,* and obbligato to accompany class songs

- play recorders, keyboards, or mallet instruments from notation on chart or chalkboard

- select and play familiar melodies with I-IV-V^7-I structure, with teacher's help

- discuss how conductors communicate musical ideas to performers; practice conducting gestures and conduct duple and triple meters

- recognize D.C., D.S., repeat signs and their effect on formal structure

- select and perform folk dance from culture being studied in social studies class

Creating

Objectives

During the intermediate grades the student will:

■ use existing melodic materials to alter and produce new melodic material

■ improvise simple accompaniments to familiar melodies on pitched instruments such as xylophones, bells, Autoharp, keyboard, electronic equipment, synthesizer, and sequencer

■ create a variety of rhythmic accompaniments to familiar melodies

■ modify stylistic characteristics to create different expressive ideas

■ compose original pieces using environmental, electronic, or invented sound sources

■ invent graphic notation to represent electronic or invented sound sources

■ create dramatization to demonstrate music's mood or program

Possible Procedures

■ after teacher presents models or samples, practice altering melody by changing melodic or rhythmic pattern

■ practice and experiment with variety of accompanying styles: chordal, bass line, rhythmic pattern

■ use mallet instruments or other percussion instruments to play personal patterns to accompany selected pieces

■ alter mood of piece by changing tempo or mode using varying instruments and electronic equipment

■ construct theme and variations from "found" sounds, such as keys dropping, glass breaking, paper rustling, water dripping

■ make group decisions about how to represent time values, pitch alterations

■ select music that tells story or represents mood to act out or mime

Listening/Describing

Objectives

During the intermediate grades the student will:

■ listen to and discuss components of selected compositions

     Pitch: tonality, major/minor, atonal, cadences, steps/skips, chromatic, scalar

     Duration: tempo, patterns, syncopation, duple/triple, time signatures, alla breve or cut time, fermatas, Grand Pause

     Loudness: loud/soft, gradations, crescendo, decrescendo, accents, fortissimo, pianissimo

     Timbre: instrumental and vocal families, individual instruments and voices, electronic and folk genres

     Texture: combinations of instruments, solo/tutti, layered, terraced

     Form: canon, fugue, theme and variations, ABA, rondo, march, da capo

     Style: historical, cultural

■ move body or limbs to demonstrate understanding of rhythm and tempo

■ notate simple pitch and duration patterns from dictation

■ begin developing a repertoire of recognized masterworks and their composers, including orchestral, choral, and operatic works, and Broadway musicals

■ discuss music in own words, and, when possible, using musical vocabulary

Possible Procedures

■ Select classroom recordings of short compositions or selections to demonstrate particular components of music; listen to teacher- or student-selected music and identify component characteristics

     make chart or map to represent pitch, duration, or other component treatments

     identify musical components as they occur in music examples

     recognize and identify specific instruments and voices aurally

     identify instrumental and vocal combinations as thick, thin, layered, and so forth

     identify formal structures from notation and through listening

     examine music from a variety of native cultures; sing or dance to demonstrate selections

■ use conducting gestures to indicate tempo and rhythm; count beats verbally while subdividing rhythms by clapping

■ begin with familiar examples of simple melodies; relate to tonal center; use duration patterns of quarters and eighths

■ recognize musical examples of one or two composers from Baroque or later period by listening

■ choose new piece to listen to, and discuss the main features of the music with classmates; make written and/or recorded journal entries to keep in portfolio

Valuing

Objectives

During the intermediate grades the student will:

- display understanding of role of music in affecting mood and behavior in commercials, shopping centers, and other places

- display positive attitude in responses to music

- select a variety of types of music for personal listening pleasure

- discuss music preferences based on musical reasons

- develop an appreciation for variety of cultural or ethnic musical styles

- show awareness of music as a cultural phenomenon

Possible Procedures

- observe videos of television commercials, cue sound track only, then discuss use of music to enhance or to create moods

- participate freely in music classes through playing, singing, discussing, listening

- select from classroom collections that include a variety of popular and "classical" music when using listening stations

- be able to answer questions such as: Why do I like this piece of music?

- select and listen to a variety of local and national ethnic music; share with class through demonstration and discussion

- discuss songs from Civil War and other historical eras, relate to work songs, play-party songs

Level 6–8/7–9

Continued learning of music is important for all middle school students. Both physical and emotional growth make it possible for students to build on their elementary school instruction and begin to work with higher-order skills. The concept of "exploratory" courses should be applied to content and methods of teaching, not to scheduling patterns. Short-term learning (6–9 week music periods) results in long-term forgetting (27–30 weeks with no music scheduled).

General music courses should be scheduled consistently and sequentially throughout the school year in order to reinforce the skills and attitudes that are being developed. These courses should include singing; creating; listening; performing on and exploring many musical instruments, including electronic; and describing, which may include movement, abstract drawing and diagrams, traditional and original notation, and discussion. Regardless of the instructional approach selected, emphasis should be on the continued development of musical understanding through active involvement with the components of music.

Performing/Reading

Objectives

During the middle grades the student will:

- sing with appropriate posture and breath support throughout his or her singing range

- maintain part during group singing involving simple rounds, three-part canons, partner songs, partner songs with ostinato, and two-part songs with descant/countermelody and melody

- increase repertoire of folk and composed songs

- recognize changes in the adolescent voice, and how to continue singing through use of appropriate ranges, head voice, and breath control

- demonstrate understanding of formal and stylistic symbols and their functions

- use a systematic means to demonstrate reading skills from treble and bass staff, indicating knowledge of pitch names on staff plus ledger lines

- accompany a three-chord melody (C, F, G) on a classroom instrument such as Autoharp, bells, guitar, or electronic keyboard

Possible Procedures

- follow teacher's model or visual aids for demonstrations of proper sitting and standing posture for singing; compare sound thus produced with that resulting from poor posture and breath support

- perform and record large and small group endeavors; follow up with discussion of the degree of success in maintaining part

- sing, alone and in groups, representative American folk, cowboy, rock, bluegrass, gospel, jazz, spiritual, blues, or country-western songs as well as representative songs of other nations and style periods.

- practice, alone and with others, vocal exercises to develop head voice, voice range, tone quality, breath control, and pitch discrimination

- perform original or composed pieces in small ensembles from notation that includes expressive symbols for dynamics and tempo or formal construction such as repeat signs, da capo, dal segno, accidentals, fermata, ties, slurs, crescendo, diminuendo, forte, piano, and other dynamic markings

- perform from notation in both treble and bass clef, vocally or on classroom instruments

- play chordal accompaniment of block or broken chords (I-IV-V^7-I) for familiar pieces

Objectives

Possible Procedures

- read and perform notated rhythm patterns, including whole note, half note, quarter note, pairs of eighth notes, four sixteenth, and dotted quarter and eighth note with quarter note receiving one beat

- recognize visually from notation similar and contrasting sections or phrases

- sing or play selections that include examples of patterns, in score or charts

- select familiar pieces and then identify like and unlike sections and phrases; mark scores or sheet music with icons or A and B to codify

Creating

Objectives

During the middle grades the student will:

- improvise melodic patterns in a twelve-bar blues form

- improvise simple accompaniment using familiar melody

- use traditional and/or nontraditional notation as a means of recording and retrieving musical ideas

- create compositions using nontraditional sounds such as environmental, electronic, or created sources

- use repetition and contrast to organize a variety of components into coherent form

Possible Procedures

- using blues scale, perform created ideas instrumentally or vocally

- select instrumental or vocal recording or computer-generated theme; accompany on keyboard, guitar, or pitched mallet instruments by ear

- compose piece using real notation or icons, mixing traditional and environmental sounds; combine computer, synthesizer, and printer to record musical ideas

- improvise or compose simple pieces or phrases using environmental or electronic sounds; develop tape loops of actual or distorted "found" sounds, or use synthesized or sampled sound

- alter the phrase order of familiar ABA melody, and listen and discuss the effectiveness of each example; listen and discover how a repeated rhythm pattern can sustain interest over a period of time in works such as "Hall of the Mountain King" from Grieg's *Peer Gynt* or *Boléro* by Ravel

Listening/Describing

Objectives

During the middle grades the student will:

■ maintain attention while listening to extended music selection; identify elements or components of music aurally and visually, for example:

Pitch: tonal, atonal, major/minor, modal, intervals, harmonic progressions
Duration: duple/triple meter, tempo, pattern combinations, syncopation, ties, fermatas, complex meters
Loudness: crescendo, decrescendo, sforzando, pianissimo, attacks, dynamic changes
Timbre: instrumental and vocal families, genre representations (folk, Oriental), electronically generated altering techniques (vibrato, *col legno*)

Texture: combinations of instruments, thick and thin—solo and tutti, layered, terraced, monophonic, homophonic, polyphonic

Form: canon, fugue, sonata, ABA, concerto, theme and variations, rondo, march
Style: historical, cultural, instrumental, vocal, ethnic, geographic, nationalistic

■ aurally identify a composition or section as belonging to a historical period

■ use a standard notation score to guide listening

■ compare and contrast interpretations of the same composition

Possible Procedures

■ select recordings of extended sections of movements as examples of components of music; follow listening maps to identify components

identify characteristics of components and make call chart to represent pitch, duration, etc. Select component to concentrate on while listening to sections of compositions: pitch (understanding of tonal center, melodic and harmonic alterations); duration (effect of tempo, meter on structure); loudness (dynamic changes and patterns)

listen to and reflect on examples of Baroque solo/tutti concertos

select late Romantic composition (such as Berlioz' *Symphonie fantastique*); examine idée fixe and trace throughout; compare musical style to literature (Poe, Coleridge), visual art (Dali, Duchamp)

■ identify components that help place composition in specific historical period; collect examples for demonstrations of same; discuss and compare excerpts

■ follow overhead transparencies with highlighted themes, key changes, tempo changes, and repeats

■ provide recordings of popular adaptations, such as synthesized commercials or cartoons, to compare and contrast

continued

Objectives

During the middle grades the student will:

- create movement patterns or visual art to indicate musical structure

- expand musical vocabulary to use in analyzing music

Possible Procedures

- express repetition and contrast through selected movement or dance patterns; use color (paint, felt pieces) to indicate repetition and harmonic movement in piece

- discuss personal choices of music and analyze components using appropriate musical vocabulary such as form, dynamics, tempo

Valuing

Objectives

During the middle grades the student will:

- demonstrate awareness of music as an important part of everyday life

- choose to participate in a variety of music opportunities

- demonstrate respect for music composition as a profession

- demonstrate appropriate behavior during listening experiences

- demonstrate awareness of the affective nature of music

- express enjoyment in performing music, in both formal and informal settings

- listen to a wide variety of music for own personal pleasure

Possible Procedures

- report on music and its effects in film, television, and drama, in shopping malls, and on telephones; discuss music's presence in and absence from such places

- record personal experiences with music in journals or diaries, indicating experiences available to age group

- research and report on "favorite" famous composer, including such information as historical era, reflection of political and social atmosphere, patronage, church influence, personal sacrifices of composer, and cultural or ethnic attributes

- discuss varieties of listening experiences and audience responses during different settings, and reasons for differing responses

- discuss personal experiences with affective nature of music

- select community groups to perform with, or gather group of fellow students to play in small ensembles; play alone for personal pleasure or for others

- share personal preferences, expressing musical and nonmusical reasons

High School
General Music 9–12

General music at the high school level is offered to students who choose not to participate in school performing groups, yet who are interested in and wish to know more about music.[1] In some cases, students choose a general music course to be the course that fulfills a graduation requirement in fine arts. A few students who participate in performing groups may also wish to know more about the general aspects of music.

High school general music should provide opportunities for performing, listening, creating, and valuing music. These experiences can be used to build a variety of instructional settings or courses to provide students with content, hands-on practice, and research opportunities that can form the foundations for making informed judgments about music. General music instructional settings may include: Basic Musicianship (making music); History and Literature (appreciation/listening); Theory/Composition (writing/analysis); and Fine Arts or Humanities (music in combination with other subjects). These settings may overlap one another; for example, making music is essential to understanding and internalizing the concepts of music, listening to music is essential to knowing music, and exploring composition or arranging is important for expressing musical ideas. Technology can provide more experiences for all levels of students as they compose, store, experiment with, and retrieve their own music.

Objectives are listed here as a core of experiences from which appropriate objectives may be selected according to the desired instructional setting.[2] This collection of objectives, grouped according to Performing/Reading, Creating, Listening/Describing, and Valuing headings, may be used as a collection of sample objectives for any instructional setting for high school general music. In order to provide a balanced learning experience, objectives should be selected from each group of objectives.

---

1. *Music in the High School: Current Approaches to Secondary General Music Instruction* (Reston, VA: Music Educators National Conference, 1989).
2. *Promising Practices: High School General Music* (Reston, VA: Music Educators National Conference, 1990).

Performing/Reading

Objectives

During a general music course the student will:

■ continue further development of the ability to produce music using the voice or an instrument in small groups or individually

■ continue to develop reading skills and use of music notation

■ play and/or sing examples of scales, intervals, and chords as they occur in the musical examples studied and composed

■ demonstrate simple conducting technique through score reading

■ perform arrangements and compositions written by members of the class

■ aurally and visually analyze simple harmonic passages such as I-IV-V^7-I; I-IV-I-V^7-I

■ visually recognize formal structures such as sonata, rondo, fugue, theme and variations, waltz, march, and others

Possible Procedures

■ explore and experiment with classroom instruments, piano or keyboard labs, guitar or ukulele labs, electronic equipment including synthesizers and computers

■ explore a variety of approaches to reading notation; follow a printed score; participate in directed experiences with highlighted themes, harmonic movement, rhythm patterns on overhead transparencies, chart, or computer program

■ select brief sections as examples of scale or chord patterns; produce scale or broken chord patterns vocally or on an instrument

■ practice from simple score, noting themes, rhythm shifts, climaxes, and dynamics

■ sing or play in small group ensembles to demonstrate and analyze classroom efforts; share with class for discussion

■ use charts, graphs, or highlighted scores to trace harmonic progressions in selected pieces

■ examine a variety of scores to identify form; then discuss those elements that determine composers' decisions such as when to repeat phrases or sections or when to change key

Creating

Objectives

During a general music course the student will:

■ improvise simple instrumental accompaniments for instruments such as keyboards, guitar, Autoharp, or synthesizer, or ethnic instruments such as banjo, ukulele, or steel drums

■ create, perform, and notate simple, short compositions for voices and/or instruments

■ arrange simple pieces of music for instruments, voices, or synthesizers

■ improvise a solo around a familiar melody vocally or instrumentally

■ create dramatic interpretation of selected music

Possible Procedures

■ practice standard blues progression for students to work with in small groups to develop improvisation; use "lead-sheet" that indicates I and V^7 chords to create accompaniment

■ devise a simple melody on recorder or mallet instrument using pentatonic or dorian scale; create a melody to accompany a four-line poem; create melody that is then harmonized and arranged for small ensembles or synthesizer

■ select simple canon for experimentation with arranging; or develop a three-part arrangement of a folk-song melody

■ examine a key, scale, or simple harmonic progression to determine tonal center and chord members; follow by creating a simple improvisation on the progression

■ use movement and/or narration to depict historical events related to selected music

Listening/Describing

Objectives

During a general music course the student will:

- hear, identify, and describe the basic components of music

    Pitch: tonal, atonal, major/minor, modal, intervals, harmonic progressions, serial techniques, chromatics, enharmonics, quarter tones

    Duration: duple/triple, tempo, pattern combinations, syncopation, ties, fermatas, complex meters, subdivisions, absence of pulse

    Loudness: crescendo, decrescendo, sforzando, pianissimo, attacks, subito, dynamic changes, meno, mosso, piu

    Timbre: instrumental and vocal families; genre representations such as folk, Oriental, scat, bluegrass; electronically generated altering techniques such as double stops of "prepared" piano

    Texture: combinations of instruments' pitch ranges, thick and thin—solo/tutti, layered, monophonic, homophonic, polyphonic

    Form: canon, fugue, sonata, concerto, theme and variation, rondo, march, oratorio, opera

    Style: historical, cultural, instrumental, vocal, ethnic, geographic, nationalistic, popular, classical

- identify social and political events that affect the style of composers

Possible Procedures

- Identify components while listening to familiar selections; indicate selected components on chart or map

    Compare excerpts from a Bach chorale with a Berg piece to reflect on use of pitch organizations

    discuss how changes in tempo alter the expressive quality of a piece

    use correct terms to indicate volume levels of Tchaikovsky's *1812 Overture*

    listen to and compare vocal sounds of a "country" singer and an Oriental singer, or an opera singer and a singer of popular music

    sing a single-line melody and then add a guitar accompaniment to illustrate monophonic and homophonic texture

    discuss how formal structure also reflects historical style of a composition

    develop time line indicating composers, compositions, and concurrent events during early American history; compare and contrast music from a variety of cultures (western, nonwestern)

- report on the influence of American jazz on the music of composers such as Ravel, Debussy, Stravinsky, Milhaud, and Bernstein

Objectives	Possible Procedures

- use correct vocabulary to describe and discuss musical experiences

- describe major historical eras in music and how they may be characterized

- explore role of music in society, past and present

- discuss elements of music using appropriate terminology

- listen to examples of different historical styles of music and discuss stylistic differences

- research and report on examples of humor in music and how it reflects the political, social, and/or musical style of that period

Valuing

Objectives

During a general music course the student will:

- develop an awareness of the aesthetic qualities in music

- identify, describe, and discuss various career and avocational opportunities available in music

- compare and contrast relationship of music and other art forms—dance, theater, visual art, and literature

- attend a variety of local musical events

- demonstrate appropriate audience behavior for a variety of performance situations

- exhibit interest in personal musical heritage as it relates to family, community, or country

- select from a variety of music for personal listening pleasure

- explore the affective nature of music, the psychological implications for listeners

- explore the variety of music and how it reflects cultural and ethnic traits

Possible Procedures

- develop sensitivity to the expressive qualities of music and describe the components that contribute to aesthetic qualities

- select a musician and develop a profile of that individual, including private study, practice, promotion, and recording techniques

- record personal experiences with related arts or multimedia events such as musical productions (*Cats, Phantom of the Opera*), movies (*West Side Story, Showboat*), and MTV productions

- use class-prepared outline to identify performance components; write a mini-review of performance

- after attending a performance, report on audience behavior and how it contributed to or detracted from the performance

- conduct personal interviews with family members, community members, or local performers to discover roots of personal musical heritage

- keep journal of personal favorites, representing different eras, styles, and genres; collect recordings that exhibit interest in variety

- prepare a report on how music is used to help sell products or ideas

- select and discuss ethnic music from another culture; discuss similarities and differences of instruments, style, rhythms